SERIES EDITOR: DONALD SOMME

OSPREY MODELLING MANU

PANZERKAMPFWAGEN III

RODRIGO HERNÁNDEZ CABOS

AND

JOHN PRIGENT

First published in Great Britain in 2001 by Osprey Publishing, Elms Court,
Chapel Way, Botley, Oxford OX2 9LP United Kingdom
Email: info@ospreypublishing.com

ISBN 1 84176 208 3

Editor: Donald Sommerville
Design: Compendium Publishing Ltd

Originated by Accion Press
Printed in China through World Print Ltd

01 02 03 04 05   10 9 8 7 6 5 4 3 2 1

For a Catalogue of all books published by Osprey Military and Aviation
please write to:
The Marketing Manager, Osprey Publishing Ltd., P.O. Box 140,
Wellingborough, Northants NN8 4ZA United Kingdom
Email: info@ospreydirect.co.uk

The Marketing Manager, Osprey Direct USA,
c/o Motorbooks International, PO Box 1,
Osceola, WI 54020-001, USA
Email: info@ospreydirectusa.com

www.ospreypublishing.com

Acknowledgements

The Introduction and Chapters 3 to 7 were written by John Prigent.

Chapter 1 is by Sergio Usera Mugica, José A. Mayoralas Fernández and Rodrigo Hernández Cabos. Chapter 2 is by Miguel Jiménez Martín, with assistance in model making and painting from Jorge López Ferrer and Ana Estrella Marcos.

Translation from Spanish by Y2K Translations.

The walkround photographs were taken by Rodrigo Hernández Cabos and Octavio Diaz Camara.
Scale Drawings: Carlos de Diego Vaquerizo.
Colour side views: Rodrigo Hernández Cabos.
Model for illustrating the cover: Rodrigo Hernández Cabos and Sergio Usera Mugica.
Photographs selected by: Accion Press, S.A.
The publisher's acknowledge with gratittude the help given by the following museums: Musée des Blindés "Général Estienne" de Saumur, and Bovington Tank Museum.

CONTENTS

INTRODUCTION

BELOW **Here is a Panzer III Ausf. G showing its external gun mantlet and short 5cm gun. It still has the first types of sprocket and idler wheel.**

BOTTOM **This is an Ausf. E in North Africa, used as a command tank by 21st Panzer Division. Here you can see very clearly the shape of the 3.7cm gun recoil housing and the internal gun mantlet with two coaxial machine guns.**

BRIEF HISTORY OF THE PANZER III

The Panzerkampfwagen III was the first 'proper' tank design of Hitler's Germany. (*Panzerkampfwagen* translates literally as 'armoured fighting vehicle'.) In March 1935 Germany had repudiated the part of the Treaty of Versailles which banned production of tanks, though the Panzers I and II had been designed earlier and were in production as 'agricultural tractors'. These two were intended for training and reconnaissance respectively rather than combat use, but the Panzer III was to be have a gun capable of defeating opposing tanks.

The *Ausführung* (loosely meaning 'version' and usually abbreviated to Ausf.) A went into production in 1936 under the title of *Zugführerwagen* or ZW. The term meant 'platoon leader's vehicle' and was intended as a security measure, but it remained in use at the factory, with a number to distinguish production batches, until the last PzKpfw III was built in 1943. The Ausf. A to D used four trial suspensions with external springs. Only limited numbers of these first four sub-types were built, but full-scale production was started in 1939 with the Ausf. E which had a newly designed torsion bar suspension using six medium-sized road-wheels.

The Ausf. E and F used a 3.7cm gun with an internal mantlet and two coaxial machine guns, but this was soon replaced by a more powerful 5cm gun with an external mantlet and only one machine gun to produce the Ausf. G. The same gun was used on the last Ausf. Fs and retrofitted

to some Ausf. Es, but in its turn it was found lacking and replaced by a longer 5cm gun to produce the Ausf. J. Meanwhile the Ausf. H had introduced the wider track and new sprocket and idler, needed to carry the extra weight of the additional armour which had been found necessary. There was no Ausf. I, and the Ausf. K designation was used for a command tank with extra radio equipment. The next main version was therefore the Ausf. L, distinguished by its spaced armour, added in front of the driver's position and to the gun mantlet.

The Ausf. M was designed to be able to ford rivers too deep for the earlier versions, and had special sealable hatches for its air intakes and outlets together with a snorkel arrangement to stop water flooding down its exhaust pipes. By this time the Panzer III's 5cm gun was of little use against the T-34s and KV-1s it was meeting on the Russian Front, and the Panzer IV was taking its place as the main German gun tank. The final Panzer III, the Ausf. N, was therefore modified to carry a short 7.5cm gun which allowed it to fire high explosive shells at infantry strong-points, machine gun nests and anti-tank gun positions. In fact a number of Ausf. Ns were allotted to Tiger battalions for exactly that purpose. Many Ausf. Ls, Ms and Ns had skirt armour added to their hulls and turrets.

The Panzer III was also used for several special-purpose designs. Special command tanks were produced on Ausf. D, E and H hulls with extra radios, a dummy gun mounted in a fixed standard turret bolted to the hull, and in most cases a conspicuous 'bedstead' radio aerial fixed around the engine deck. Late command tanks used a 'star' aerial, looking like a normal rod aerial with a spray of smaller ones round its top. This was much less obvious and made the command tanks harder for an enemy to pick out for attention.

Other special-purpose PzKpfw IIIs were the flamethrower tanks built on Ausf. M hulls. They looked very similar to the normal gun tanks but had a thicker flame tube instead of the usual gun barrel. *Tauchpanzer*, or 'diving tanks' were also produced with special sealing arrangements to

ABOVE **An Ausf. G of the *Afrika Korps* shows this version's squarer gun recoil housing very clearly. Compare this with the photograph of the Ausf. E command tank at bottom left and the difference is obvious.**

ABOVE **These tanks are Ausf. Js seen in Russia. The second-type engine deck overhang and improved commander's cupola are well-shown, and you can see how the stowage box completely hides the turret rear shape. However, it can still be distinguished as the improved turret rear plate because its joint with the sides is at the same angle as the side of the turret door, while the early turret rear showed a marked angle forward at this joint.**

let them cross rivers completely submerged, using a floating snorkel to obtain fresh air for the crew and engine.

Nearly all versions of the Panzer III gun tank and several of the variants are available as models. The differences between them, some subtle and some very obvious, make for a fascinating series of models showing how the design developed. The famous Sturmgeschütz III and other self-propelled guns using the chassis of the Panzer III will be the subject of a future book in this series.

PANZER III MODELS THEN AND NOW

Until quite recently the Panzer III modeller has been poorly served with little choice. Tamiya produced a 1/35 scale late-type Panzer III in the late 1970s, with features that were really a mixture of Ausf. J, L and M, and flexible 'rubber band' tracks which were not very well detailed. This made it adaptable to any of those sub-types with a little work, and built straight from the box it was a fair representation of a tank rebuilt in base workshops and upgraded with later parts. Although it can still sometimes be found it cannot be recommended to modellers today, as modern moulding techniques have far surpassed its level of detail.

In the smaller scales there was a 1/76 Panzer III Ausf. L from Matchbox, a nice little model with good detail for its scale though the flexible tracks left something to be desired. It came with a moulded polystyrene base with a few accessories which made an instant diorama.

Revell has recently issued a 1/72 scale PzKpfw III Ausf. L, available with or without Panzergrenadier figures, and this appears to be produced from the Matchbox moulds even though it is marked as a different scale. Esci also produced a Panzer III in 1/72 scale, this time the Ausf. M and also quite good for its size, but this seems to have disappeared from the market. In 1/48 scale Bandai made a PzKpfw III Ausf. M kit, but although some of the Bandai kits have been reissued under the Fuman label this one does not seem to be among them yet.

In the late 1980s Gunze Sangyo produced two 1/35 scale kits, of the PzKpfw III Ausf. J and L, and of the Ausf. N, both labelled as 'high-tech' because they included etched metal parts and white metal castings as well as separate track links. They were expensive but did build into good models, so good that many of the later Dragon kits actually used the Gunze Sangyo moulds for their main parts.

Over the last few years the Panzer III has seen a renaissance in 1/35 scale, with fine kits coming from Dragon and Tamiya. Looking at the latter first, Tamiya has used state-of-the-art techniques to produce a superb model of the Ausf. L with excellent detail. Its tracks are the flexible type, but highly detailed and moulded in a new plastic which can be stuck with ordinary liquid polystyrene cement. Etched metal exterior improvement sets and a resin interior are available for this kit.

Dragon has launched out with a series of Panzer III kits, all nicely done and depicting different Ausf.en very well. Some have been reboxed by Revell under a co-production arrangement for sale in Europe. They come with link-to-link plastic tracks, which some modellers do not like due to the time needed to assembly them. However, they do allow the typical sag of a German tank's tracks to be shown easily. So far Dragon has produced the Ausf. E as used in the 1940 French campaign, in 1941 in the Balkans and Russia and by the *Afrika Korps* in 1941–2, the Panzer III (Fl) which was the flamethrower version distinguished by the untapered flame tube which replaces the standard tapered gun barrel, the Panzer III Ausf. G, the Panzer Befehlswagen III Ausf. H, which was the command tank built on an Ausf. H chassis, the Ausf. J control tank for Borgward radio-controlled chargelaying vehicles, and a single kit allowing construction of either the Ausf. M or the Ausf. N. This is quite an array, and mix-and-match use of these kits will allow the building of almost any Panzer III from the Ausf. E onward.

Dragon kits have a tendency to go out of production for a while and then reappear either under the Dragon or the associated Shanghai Dragon labels, but any of them will build a good model and all are worth getting whenever they appear. Dragon produces two separate track sets for Panzer IIIs, an early version and a superdetailed late type, and there are hosts of etched metal sets to fit these kits too. It is worth mentioning that, while Dragon's kits include etched metal grilles for the engine air intakes, these are not always included in the re-releases by Shanghai Dragon and Revell. The plastic versions of the grilles are acceptable but do not give the same appearance to this rather conspicuous feature, so it is worth buying a separate grille set if one is not included.

ABOVE **Tamiya's original Panzer III kit, number 35011, appeared in 1971 and included the guns for both the Ausf. M and Ausf. N – some Ns having been built on Ausf. M chassis. It was intended for motorisation so had some compromises with scale appearance, plus holes for the battery, switch etc. The kit was issued both with and without the electric motor and gearbox and the extra figures shown on the box were included.**

PANZER III AUSF. J & L

The famous Japanese firm of Gunze Sangyo manufactures two kits of the Panzer III: one which can make the J or the L versions and one for the Ausf. N. The standard of both is high, even though the kits have been on the market for some time. Despite the fact that they have been designed with the emphasis on quality, the models are not perfect and will benefit from being finished off with etched-metal sets from other makers and some scratch-built parts. The kit for the Ausf. J or L version is the basis for the various sections of this chapter.

The basics tools for our model: the Gunze Sangyo kit and the *Achtung Panzer* reference book.

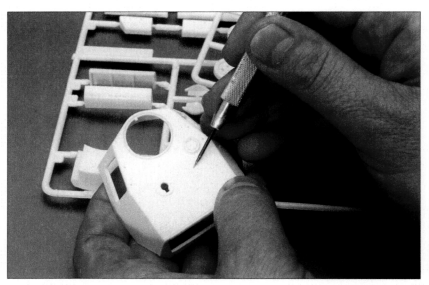

Detail of the many screws located in the roof of the turret which are reproduced with exceptional quality.

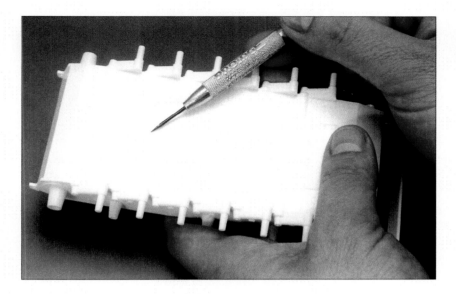

MAKING THE MODEL

The kit contains a mixture of metal and plastic parts of various types. In case you have never handled a kit of this type before, what are the differences between these and earlier models? We will attempt to clarify the details point by point.

Plastic Injection Moulded Parts

The plastic injection moulded parts reproduce the smallest detail and can show the rivets, screws and other tiny features. The outline of the track guards is reproduced to perfect scale and the underside of the vehicle is as profusely detailed as any other part.

Cast Metal Parts

There a great many of these, such as driving and tensioning wheels and their couplings to the chassis, lights, hatches and others, and these parts

BELOW LEFT **Two etched-brass frets for reproducing very small or delicate parts.**

BELOW **Two different barrels for the 5cm gun are supplied. One replicating the later 60 calibre weapon and the other the earlier 42 calibre one. These are turned in brass so that you only have to enlarge the muzzle orifice to make them ready for fitting to the model.**

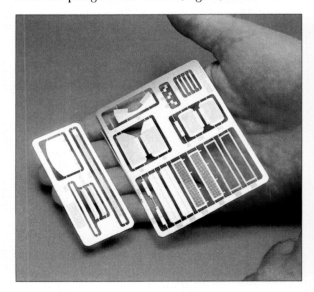

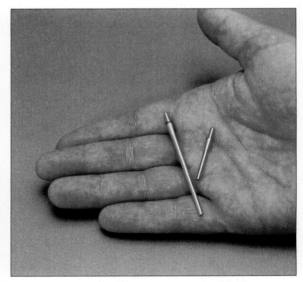

The brass gun barrel and white
metal mantlet fitted to the turret
assembly.

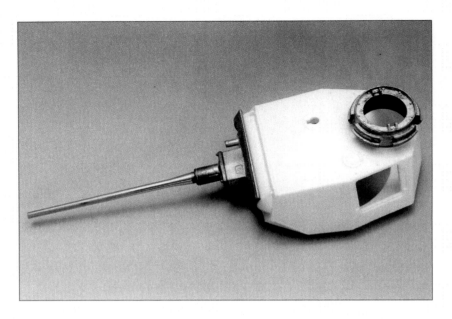

perfectly reproduce the original cast parts. Important details are the
turned brass gun barrels. The kit contains two types to choose from: a
short one made to represent the 5cm L/42 weapon, and a long one
which replicates the more powerful 5cm L/60 gun.

Etched-metal
Various very fine parts are reproduced by this method; moving parts of
the track guards, the cover of the spare parts box, ventilation grilles, etc.
As you would expect, reproduction to scale is unsurpassed. Metal parts
also include wires of various sizes and a steel cable.

Tracks
As you would expect the independent track links supplied with the kit
are of high quality, almost identical to those of the Model Kasten
accessory set.

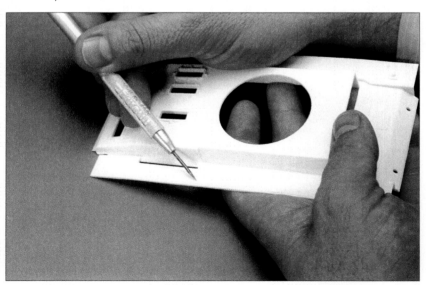

The non-slip embossing on the
track guards is so finely detailed
that it can scarcely be noticed at

a glance.

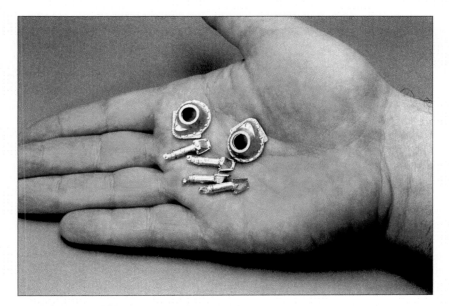

The shock absorbers and the mountings of the driving wheels are reproduced in metal, imitating the original castings perfectly.

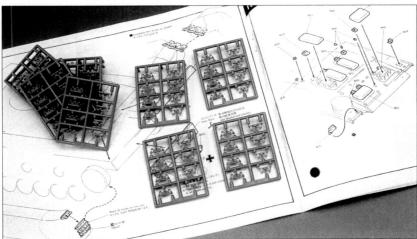

The individual track links; the only problem is that the mould marks are very apparent and it is necessary to fill them with putty.

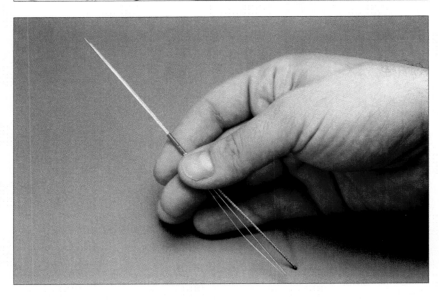

Sections of metal wire and steel cable for making various cylindrical parts are included in the kit.

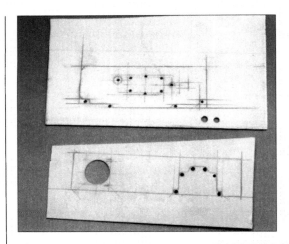

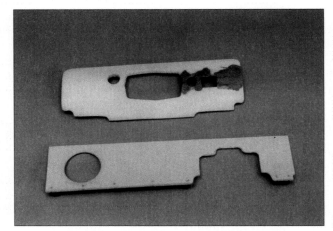

ABOVE **Pencil tracing of the extra armour plate fitted to the Ausf. L with holes drilled to enable the various necessary openings to be cut out.**

ABOVE RIGHT **Once the openings have been cut out and filed level, you need to mark out the areas for the rivets.**

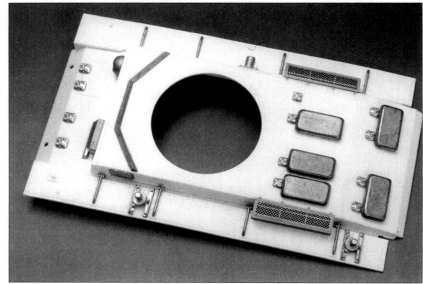

RIGHT **The top part of the hull showing the arrangement of the principal metal parts.**

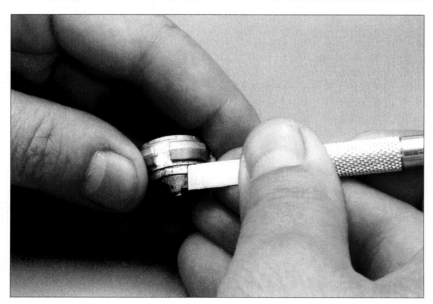

RIGHT **It is necessary to reduce the size of the ring of the commander's cupola to make it fit into the opening in the turret.**

The independent track links engage perfectly in the wheels and also exhibit the characteristic droop.

The bottom part of the hull with the shock absorbers and wheels already fitted in position.

Possible Problems

In spite of everything, there are some details that are not adequately resolved by the basic kit or by alterations to it and if we want to have a perfect model, it is necessary to add some etched-metal parts from the set produced by On The Mark Models, in particular the following: fasteners for the spare parts box, hooks and mountings for the jack and the various tools.

Other parts must be home made. These include the track guard rear support guide, made with a strip of plastic and a little putty, and the clamps for the towing cable which are the wrong shape in the kit. It is necessary to create replacements for these with a strip of metal folded with round-nosed pliers.

The cover on the turret spare parts box is etched-metal. The hinges on the locks supplied with the kit don't work and you will do better to use those supplied in the On The Mark set.

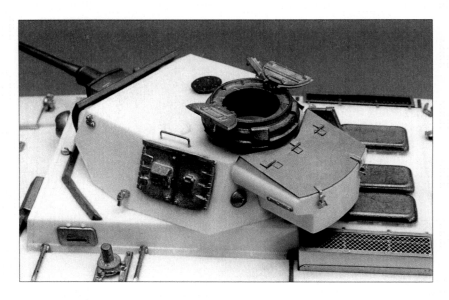

Making the Ausf. L

The extra armour fitted to this later version must be added, both for the turret and for the front of the hull, using plastic sheet of various thicknesses and Verlinden plastic rivets. Details of the method can be found in *Achtung Panzer No. 2* (see References Chapter for further details), which is in any case a highly recommended source of Panzer III information. The most difficult part of the operation is following the curvature of the armour plating of the turret, which is obtained by forcing plastic round a wooden cylinder, holding it with adhesive tape and applying heat from a drier so that the plastic adopts the shape. The exhausts are protected with a specially shaped plate which is included in the On The Mark etched-metal set, as are also the various jack mountings, shackles and clips for other tools.

Assembly

Most of the parts must be stuck with cyanoacrylate glue since all the small parts are metal. Special care is required for the 12 etched-metal pieces. One of these is a plate that must be inserted under the track guards before fitting the air intakes, since once these are fitted, it is impossible to fit this part. Another point to note is that the housing for the combat hatch is very large and it must either be made smaller or the turret opening must be enlarged.

Positioning of the front armour plate with rivets and metal brackets.

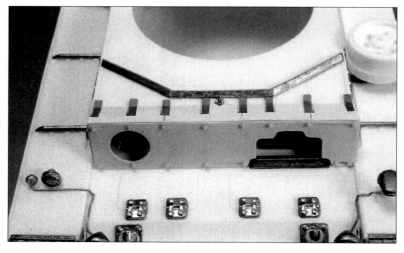

The additional armour plate added in front of the driver and the gun mantlet is made from plastic sheet 0.5mm thick, available from model shops. A pattern is traced from drawings in the *Achtung Panzer* book and

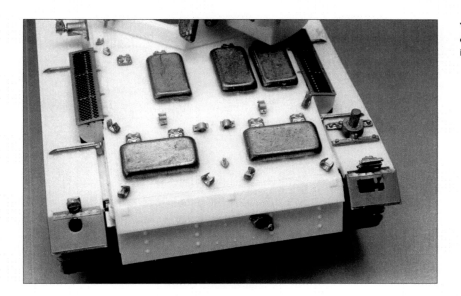

You will need to make the openings for the location lights in the rear track guards

transferred to the plastic by pricking through every corner and angle with a needle to leave marks in the plastic. These are joined up with a pencil and ruler. Holes are drilled inside the lines marking areas to be removed for openings in the armour so that these parts can be cut out with a knife without splitting the plastic. The openings are then cleaned up with a knife and file, and finally the plates are cut off the plastic sheet. The sides and top covers are made in the same way but using 0.3mm plastic sheet. The top supports for the driver's added armour are made with strips cut from the edges of the etched metal fret.

View of the completed model ready for painting. This photograph shows clearly all the different materials used.

PANZERS IN THE DESERT

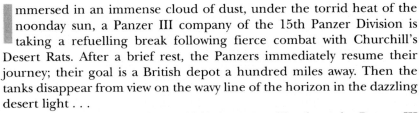

BELOW **The excellent quality of the kit allows us to open the stowage bin of the turret and to place appropriate items inside, without there being any need for adaptation.**

BOTTOM **Careful building, painting and weathering captures the appearance of a real tank in the desert.**

Immersed in an immense cloud of dust, under the torrid heat of the noonday sun, a Panzer III company of the 15th Panzer Division is taking a refuelling break following fierce combat with Churchill's Desert Rats. After a brief rest, the Panzers immediately resume their journey; their goal is a British depot a hundred miles away. Then the tanks disappear from view on the wavy line of the horizon in the dazzling desert light . . .

Throughout 1941 and into 1942, in scenes like these the Panzer III was the principal protagonist in the amazingly rapid advances made by the German armoured forces in North Africa. It was the mainstay of the tank units of the 15th and 21st Panzer Divisions that gained fame as Rommel's *Afrika Korps*.

The Model

This section deals with how to develop the model discussed in the first part of this chapter to represent just such a desert champion. The vehicle is the Ausf. J, made from the Gunze Sangyo kit and On The Mark accessory set, as already described.

The only home-produced items that we have added are various parts to provide the typical look of

German desert tanks: protective sandbags made from two-part epoxy putty and fitted to the front of the tank, giving the impression of weight; a rack for carrying fuel cans and other items of spare kit made from the remains of photo-etched items; and a different set of crew figures, as shown, contributing to the realism and attractive appearance of the tank.

The only other significant modification is to wheels and running gear. In the desert these tended to suffer a lot of damage, so we have sandpapered the edges of the rubber parts and made various slight indents with a knife to imitate this wear and tear.

Painting

Before starting to paint the Panzer III, we spent a good while carefully examining many photos of *Afrika Korps* vehicles. One conclusion very

ABOVE LEFT **The painting technique applied to the Panzer III produces subtle results, but this does not mean that the depiction of wear and tear is any less impressive.**

ABOVE **The smooth effects of the airbrush help produce the appearance of damage and the effects of light.**

LEFT **Many German tanks in North Africa were fitted with home-made racks to carry fuel and water cans. Those used for water were marked with the white cross seen here.**

quickly stood out: that the entire tank used to accumulate a whole heap of filth. The paintwork would be burnt by the sun, there was dust, dirt particles and grime to spare, shown in our model in the form of washes or smears of tones that are lighter or darker than the base colour. This effect was particularly prevalent on vertical surfaces or those that were slightly sloping. To all of this can be added, for tanks that had been involved in earlier campaigns in Europe, the remains of Panzer grey paintwork appearing on edging and in corners where the desert over-painting might wear away.

In order to paint a tank with all these details and at the same time to give its bulky shapes profile, bringing out highlights and shaded areas, the best thing is to use a range of techniques to achieve different effects. The danger that you face is one of mixing up the results of all these; to avoid this, we used paints of different types. In addition, you need to work with small brushes and apply each technique carefully tank part by tank part. You have to avoid rough finishes — the imitation of a crude appearance is not achieved through the employment of crude methods.

The process we used was the following:

Base paint
Tamiya desert sand colour ref. XF-29 (acrylic) applied with an airbrush.

Shading
Darkening the base colour with dark brown we provided shading for all the tank's corners and cracks as if we were panelling an aircraft. However, we also lightened the base colour in other areas to bring out highlights on those surfaces and in those areas where the most light would be reflected, but always being careful to avoid creating too much contrast. When using this technique, we again used Tamiya acrylic paint heavily diluted with thinner from the same company. Acrylic tones used for airbrushing can also serve us here.

Washes
We made a mixture that was very rich in thinner (90%) using paints soluble in turpentine (including oils). As this mixture has turpentine as its solvent, it will not affect the shading with acrylic paints undertaken during the previous phase. Our washes included a very dark brown colour (almost black) applied very selectively, with a fine brush, to rivets, joints and corners of the tank.

Once this stage is complete the detail on the model will be more sharply in profile, meaning it will stand out more.

Blending

This was carried out using a mixture of paint and thinner (30% and 70%, respectively) applied to the surfaces of the tank, part by part, with a fine brush, spreading it rapidly with pure thinner using downward brush strokes. This was carried out first using light sand colour and the operation was then repeated, more selectively, using a dark brown colour. The purpose of this blending process is to imitate the smears of dirt that we mentioned above.

TOP LEFT **Blending is used to imitate the different sorts of wear and tear that was typically found on desert tanks.**

TOP RIGHT **The wear and tear is accentuated more on the vertical surfaces by using blending to create stains going in a downward direction; the airbrush also plays a part in this work.**

ABOVE LEFT **The general aspect of the model offers both a wealth of masses and shapes, and wear and tear to the paintwork that is smooth in effect but clearly evident.**

ABOVE RIGHT **The outcome from combining painting techniques: shaded areas and highlights, wear and tear and dirt.**

LEFT **The typical sag of German tank tracks is captured here. Another very common feature of German tanks in the desert was for the crew to link together their water bottles and hang them on the back of the turret bin.**

RIGHT **Tanks in the desert were rarely seen not carrying extra kit. Including such items allows the modeller to introduce different colours from those used on the rest of the model and to break the monotony.**

Once again paints soluble in turpentine should be used for this process.

Dry brushing
This familiar technique was the next stage, using a very light sand colour, applied very smoothly over the whole tank, but especially on edges and projecting items. However, as a result of the careful application of the techniques covered earlier, the dry brush loses much of its usual role in this model; it is only on the lower parts that this technique is used to any large extent.

Remains of earlier paintwork
Our Panzer III shows the remains of old Panzer grey paintwork. To imitate this effect, using a very fine brush, we applied small portions of

BELOW **Superstition is not forgotten, as shown by the horseshoe painted on the turret. Panzer grey shows through principally in the nooks and crannies that the later paint could not reach, beneath each scratch and mark of friction, and on nearly all the edges.**

the colour to those parts most exposed to friction as well as to the corners, proceeding to blur the edges with thinner in order to eliminate the hardness and intensity of this dark colour.

Other final touches

The exhaust pipes, engine ventilator grilles and gun muzzles all tended to have dark stains left around them after long use and service. If we apply very diluted black paint with an airbrush, we achieve the effect that we are looking for.

Tracks

These have a dark chocolate base colour with black washes and are finished by a final dry-brush application with a metallic colour over the parts of them that would be most exposed to wear and tear.

Varnishing

Once the tank is complete, we add a matt varnish. Using this will allow us to avoid getting any unwanted shine or reflections that would otherwise probably be produced by our use of paints of different types. Throughout the entire process you can keep correcting excesses or defects in the work you produce.

ABOVE **Overall view of the completed model**

PERSONALISING A PANZER III AUSF. L

The Panzer III saw action in many theatres, with many units and many camouflage schemes all of which are very well documented photographically. This means it is easy to 'personalise' — to add sufficient detail through painting that ensure your model is clearly distinguishable from anybody else's model of the same tank.

RIGHT **The supports for the equipment boxes were made with spare pieces of the photo-etched fret. The boxes themselves were assembled with plastic sheet and Evergreen plastic strips.**

LEFT **The wooden handle of the shovel has two tones of acrylic colour: brown red as a base with golden brown.**

BELOW **The spare parts boxes were dirtied with washes of brown and beige, applying beige with a dry brush over the wash and dusting with an airbrush with very dilute and smooth desert yellow.**

RIGHT **Ammunition boxes and canvas rolls are part of a resin kit from Verlinden, painted with Vallejo acrylic.**

BELOW **The colour scheme chosen was used in the first half of 1943; the grey is combined with irregular green bands and patches of dark yellow.**

The model discussed in this section is a Panzer III Ausf. L, typical of those in action on the Eastern Front during the early summer of 1943.

Colour Scheme

In the spring of 1943, after removing the white winter camouflage, the German tanks were left with their old panzer grey. At that time a new camouflage pattern was introduced based on olive green patches or broad stripes added on top of the old paintwork.

The great offensive against the Kursk salient, in June 1943, was one of the largest tank battles of the war, involving huge numbers of German tanks. The latest models had a new colour scheme using green and brown on an ochre base (see Camouflage section, page 55). Older armoured vehicles, formerly painted in grey and green, were painted in the field and given brown patches.

Additional kit

Many personal variations can be introduced on our model, reflecting the variations put in place by the real-life Panzer crews. Given the limited space they had available inside, they made extensive use of the sides and engine covers of their vehicles for carrying various extras. One of the most widely used additions was

ABOVE **The tracks were painted with coffee brown A-82 acrylic and washed with black then given a touch with a dry brush of metallic 'steel' enamel.**

BELOW **The photo-etched metal has the finest details, such as the mounting for the jack, with its straps and brackets.**

some strips of metal welded on the rear part of the hull, to form a support for equipment boxes. As this type of addition was not standardised, there were innumerable variations. Looking at photographs of these vehicles, you can find all kinds of additions, from boxes, rolls of canvas, blankets or bundles, to baskets of pork sausages or other meats.

Verlinden offers many kits with perfectly usable canvas rolls and ammunition boxes which can be employed in whatever combination you

By combining the Gunze Sangyo kit and an additional etched metal set from On The Mark Models, we obtain a final result that is possibly approaching perfection.

wish. However, provided you have time, it is equally possible and probably more rewarding to scratch-build certain types of baggage, such as bundles, of the exact size. Epoxy putty is a good material to use. It is easy to handle and shapes itself well to the surfaces on which it is fixed, thus giving the impression of weight.

Modelling should be done in two stages. First make up a quantity of the approximate size you are going to need. Then mark in the grooves for the ropes that will hold the bundle to the tank and then the creases made by them.

Once the shape has been roughly obtained, hold the item under the heat of a light bulb or gentle heater. When it sets hard, tidy up the creases and folds with a file to give it the final shape. Finally clean the whole thing with a scouring pad.

BELOW **Each colour was dry-brushed with a lighter tone of the same colour; apart from making the parts stand out, this process helps the whole model acquire an appropriate dusty appearance.**

BOTTOM **The rivets in the two appliqué armour shields were darkened with sepia colours and the streaks on the coaxial machine gun with sepia and black.**

ABOVE **The dirt on the lower parts was painted with natural dark, light brown and beige acrylic.**

ABOVE RIGHT **Roll of canvas modelled with Milliput two-part epoxy putty.**

RIGHT **The spare tracks carried on the front of the hull were painted with Vallejo red cadmium brown C-46 acrylic with a wash of black and highlighted using a dry brush with light cadmium red C-39.**

BELOW **The commander sitting in the turret is made of metal by Ara; the other figure is by Tamiya with a Hornet tunic.**

Painting

The paint scheme for the tank was done using the following Tamiya acrylic colours: Panzer grey XF-63 for the whole vehicle; olive green XF-58 patches and stripes; and dark grey XF-60 patches. The greys and green were close in tone, although different in colour, and had various shades. Inks were used to darken the screws, rivets, etc. Several coats of black wash were also applied. Using the dry brush technique, each of the colours was lightened using Vallejo acrylic: the dark grey, with light grey, S-2; and the dirty lower areas with beige B-17 and a little white. On the front and rear parts, a little dust was applied with Tamiya acrylic XF-59 desert yellow using the airbrush.

ADVANCED PROJECTS

The stunning effect of the
completed model, with the turret
tossed skywards by the blast.

This chapter deals with two more advanced projects in which first
the model itself and then the setting are carefully recreated after
much painstaking research.

The first subject is a Panzer III Ausf. G
in Africa, the second (page 40) a Panzer
III Ausf. J in Russia.

Our first model is based on the
Dragon Panzer III Ausf. G *Afrika Korps* kit
with Verlinden accessories and represents
the culmination of several years of intensive
investigation into the field of knocked-out
armoured vehicles.

To arrive at the effects of destruction shown in this
type of model, we need a good authentic photograph
on which it can be based and
also an in-depth study of all
the   physical,
historical and
visual aspects

that surround such a situation. Shown here is a complex example, but the you should not be intimidated by the thought of building a badly damaged or destroyed vehicle — especially once you have understood the processes described in this article. Our intention is to encourage you to search out appropriate reference photos and try a similar project by showing the exciting possibilities offered by this theme.

The Plan

As in the preparation for the perfect crime, we will carefully explain the fairly complex steps to be followed in building this Panzer III. We deliberately chose a model for which there are currently a wide range of accessories available (engine, gearbox, etched-metal kits, etc.) and for which a lot of visual information is published, both for the interior in its original form and for battle-damaged examples. The final model has to be of more than just visual interest to modellers; we wanted to end up with

RIGHT **In the road wheel area, ash from the burnt rubber of the tyres has been simulated.**

BELOW RIGHT **The effects of burning and destruction must not appear uniform from one area to another.**

BOTTOM RIGHT **The force of an internal explosion would often burst the engine hatches open.**

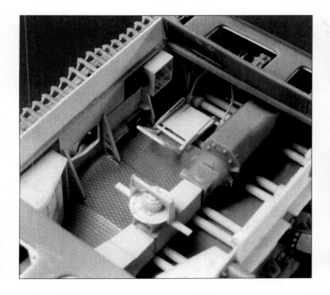
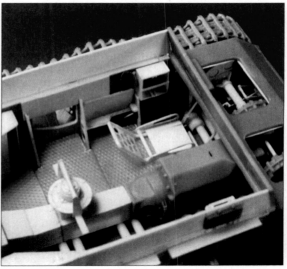

something more than a completely burned out shell with no interesting physical details. Furthermore, we wanted to show the changes that a military vehicle could suffer, forming new contorted shapes with a unique identity which could, perhaps, take on an unexpected artistic value of their own.

We started with a single photograph, so the task of imagining the parts of the vehicle that were hidden from the camera was the first difficulty. Judging what the true colours might be from a black-and-white original was also tricky. Copying the photograph accurately would mean tracing and extracting every last piece of information from the parts that could be seen to show the effects of the damage, the burnt wheels and other details. Reconstructing the interior from scratch would also be required. Some of the parts shown in the photo did not correspond to the standard German models — setting another problem. However, the photo undoubtedly provided an attractive subject, but a very challenging one if plastic and resin materials were to be used.

ABOVE & ABOVE LEFT **These views of the interior show the non-slip floor made from etched metal and the construction of the driver's seat.**

The Murder Weapon

It only remained to work out the weapon that had knocked out the vehicle in the first place — knowing this would help in calculating how the hidden aspects of the damage ought to be shown. From reference and history books it seems that most tanks damaged in this way were victims of the work of demolition groups, though at times the British heavy or anti-tank artillery produced similar results. But the fact that the tracks were intact was a sign that the vehicle had probably been put out of action from the inside — that is, by an explosion caused by a demolition group. This is very important, particularly when building the hidden side of the tank and

BELOW **Even though the model contains many detailed parts obtained from commercial accessory sets made in resin and etched metal, most of the parts forming the interior are home made.**

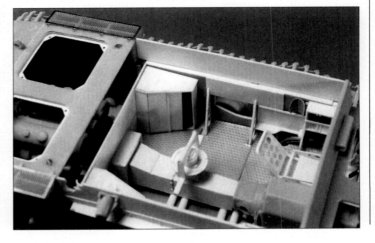

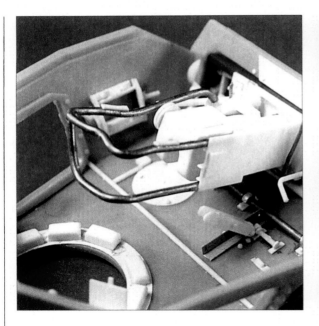

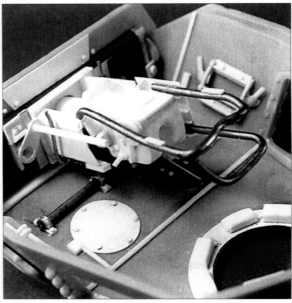

ABOVE, ABOVE RIGHT & BELOW
All the interior parts of the turret and gun must be home-made.

reconstructing the damage. The explosion that took place was sudden and very powerful, sufficient to blow the fighting compartment roof and the gun turret into the air, but it is strange that (according to our reference photo) it only did limited damage to the smaller internal parts. This explosion seems to have been followed by a huge fire that burned four-fifths of the vehicle. Our reference photo also shows some piles of ash around the wheels, so it is possible that the Panzer had only been burned three or four days before the picture was taken or the ash would have been blown away by the desert winds.

Choosing Colours

However, what is the colour of a burnt tank after three or four days? Clearly there is no specific documentation as to the exact colour of such catastrophic damage during the desert war (1942–43), but a tank burned in the same way then as it does now and at the present time we

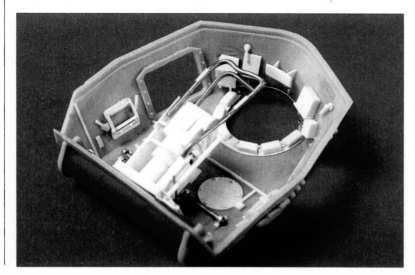

have plenty of information on burnt vehicles. It was a question of looking for and adapting such colours for our Panzer III.

Many books have been published on the wars in the Gulf, the Balkans, Somalia and elsewhere, featuring good modern colour photography which reveals the secret of painting a tank as it would be three or four days after it had burned out, something that is very different from similar charred remains after the passage of weeks or months. Chromatically speaking, this

LEFT **Detail of the wheels, drive sprocket and idlers, some of whose parts were copied in resin.**

BELOW & BOTTOM **Views of the right hand side of the hull interior, where the ammunition locker can be seen. The transmission is also carefully represented.**

variation is important. Other significant details can also be gleaned from such sources — for example it seems that sometimes the ammunition belts remaining in the interior did not completely explode.

From such evidence we reached the conclusion that the smoke effects shown in the photo could be simulated by a light, uniform coat of orange oxide, the rest of the painting being splashed with a sand colour.

This is how we chose the colours for the model: in colour photos of burnt-out tanks, whitened patches can be seen among areas turned blue by the high temperatures, along with black soot deposits and various shades of rust.

Reconstructing the Crime

For some the use of a Dragon kit, an engine and gearbox from Verlinden, a photograph from The Show Modelling, a non-slip panel from Alhambra, a gun from Jordi Rubio and a large amount of plastic, resin and silicone to make a destroyed vehicle is an extravagant crime; for us, however, it was vital in order to build a serious model of a burned-out tank. We wanted to get away from the hackneyed trick of using an old or poor quality kit to model a vehicle

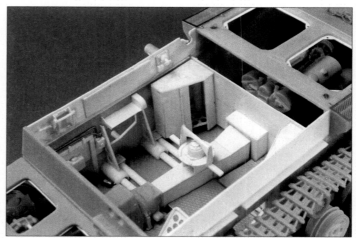

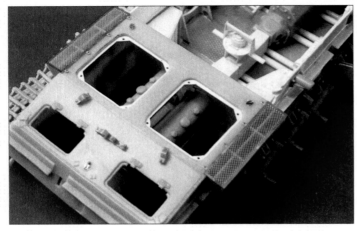

TOP **Detail of the escape hatch in one side of the hull.**

ABOVE **The panels and hatches over the engine must be left completely open.**

that has been battle-damaged — the lack of quality always shows.

The range of details incorporated in our model was far more extensive. The wheels were turned from new and copied in resin to make a complete set without tyres, including the spare wheels at the front. All the hatches will open now, as they were rebuilt with hinges. The interior of the chassis was made from Evergreen material: pedals, levers, ammunition boxes, transmission, visors, seats, etc., trying to build all of it in a manner consistent with the overall damage to the tank. This was quite a difficult task, even though there are enough kits available for detailed parts of the interior that the average model maker will have no difficulty in modifying.

The interior of the turret also had to be mainly scratch-built, including the gun mounting, sights and related equipment, and the base of the turret, which in this case had to be out in the open. On the outside, an etched-metal set was used and the tool box was reconstructed and left open. The headlights were also hollow, being made by simple vacuum forming.

Perhaps the most complicated aspect of all was adapting the position of the turret to its ring and to the roof of the fighting compartment so that it was as like the one in the photograph as possible. Also it was necessary to take into account all the little details shown in the photo — like the state of the ammunition holders, track links and minor dents that had probably occurred before the final dramatic damage, the Notek blackout driving light turned backwards and so on.

The Modelling

The painting can now proceed to the second stage, provided that we are well supported by good graphic documentation. A firm grasp of the desired final effect means that it is not just the details of painting technique and materials that give the finished result, the overall 'feel' is important. If we base ourselves firmly on the original photograph, this will show where to place a lighter or darker patch, where to put dust and where to leave ash. Keeping this idea in mind is more important than explaining what colours were used or which brush employed. The best reason for emphasising this is that, since each photograph, each tank and everybody's perception is completely different, it would not serve much purpose to give firm colour references to produce this or that effect. A model-maker who tries to build a similar model would not use

exactly the same colours and, even if he did, he might not be building a Panzer III in the desert but a Sherman, and would not know how to apply them accurately. For this reason, we believe that the manner in which new painting techniques evolve for each case should be understood without resorting to rigid rules and standards.

Nevertheless, as a general principle, blue shading, ochre washes and grey-green streaks will appear on random areas of the tank. But continue to keep in mind the final desired effect, in order to work out the best way of achieving realism, rather than simply copying these methods.

Finally, and obviously, we decided that the best way to make an authentic burned-out vehicle is to start by looking at the real thing. Consequently we took every opportunity to study colour photos, burnt scrap metal and such like. Afterwards, we had to relate what we found to paint catalogues and choose the colours that matched these references best. Lastly, please note that there are no painting techniques specified in this area of modelling; there are no magic tricks or formulae, just one solution: to copy what you see.

In this particular case, we started by airbrushing a base of different shades of brown from Tamiya. Then some smooth washes with dark Humbrol colours accentuated the dents and scratches. After that we applied the 'burnt' effects to the paintwork before turning our attention to the soot and ash deposits. We had to forget any pre-conceived ideas of how to paint a model and try to think of something new, so we did not immediately apply dry-brush effects but instead next worked with oils. Using shades of brown, sienna and blue, we applied irregular patches to the whole tank, softening some areas by overlaying thin glazes of other colours while making others sharper. We tried to emphasise the depth and contrast using blue and black tones. On the upper

ABOVE **The rear part of the hull has retained some of its paint. The damage in this area is less severe.**

ABOVE LEFT **The engine deck is not as badly damaged as the fighting compartment.**

BELOW **Engine bay details are visible through the blown-open hatches.**

areas, we applied reddish-orange tones, painting them on as streaks.

Next we painted some areas with Humbrol light grey and black to simulate the chemical changes in the paint and burned metal. We also used Humbrol paint for the rest of the original colour (streaked and spotted, German Desert Brown). Finally, we applied pastel shades to simulate the effect of ash. We sanded down a bar of black and another of white pastel colour, collected the powder with a small spatula, then deposited it irregularly over areas where there might have been inflammable material — that is, wooden handles, fabric and rubber. We started with the black powder and a mixture made up to be a very dark grey. Afterwards we applied a smaller quantity of the white powder over the black. We fixed all the powder by applying a few coats of turpentine (alternatively

TOP The gun breech and other main parts fixed inside the turret often remained in place, even when the turret was blown completely off the tank.

ABOVE The location of small accessories must appear realistic, for example the machine gun ammunition belts and ammunition boxes.

TOP RIGHT The solidly-fixed transmission stays attached, although more breakable items are hard to recognise.

RIGHT The final result is almost impossible to distinguish from a photograph of a real tank wreck.

use clear lacquer), leaving it until the solvent evaporated. Once dry, the ash was perfectly stable.

The Final Result

As can be seen, the final result is rather unusual, and achieved by avoiding standard techniques.

Some model-makers reading this section may be disconcerted to note that no colours or references or any particular methods of painting are given. But if you really want to gain anything from this section, then it is important to know that modelling is not limited to painting-by-numbers, techniques, number of colours, part numbers from etched-metal sets and interminable lists of books. Modelling is, above all, a way of interpreting reality and an attitude that transforms mere pieces of plastic and a few grams of paint into a realistic representation of a time and place.

PANZER IN THE SNOW

With the winter, the snow arrives and there is nothing better to go with this than the model we now present. This theme has been avoided by most model makers owing to the complexity and wide range that it covers though it has the potential for stunning results.

The completed model showing how, in some areas, the white paint would become damaged and thinned, and the grey base coat would show through. Different types of effects can be created to reflect this. Whitewash and even scribbled chalk were often used instead of proper paints and would wear off quickly.

The techniques involved in producing this Panzer III in winter camouflage can serve as a more general guide to dealing with the effects of
snow and other aspects of a winter scene. The average model maker who
opts for a wintry decoration usually achieves this by means of a simple
though spectacular camouflage of large regular patches, or even by
covering the whole tank with what is in effect a white blanket of some
material or other and then dirtying it by a simple traditional method.

RIGHT **The lower parts of the tank have been treated with putty and fine sand.**

BELOW **In various areas of the tank the white paint is chipped.**

This is not the approach which will be followed here. It is not that this is incorrect, however, but renowned model makers such as François Verlinden or Tony Greenland have shown that it is possible to decorate 'winter' vehicles with the most subtle camouflages so as not to destroy the accuracy of their models. This has helped us realise that there are other possibilities.

It is also certain that many winter camouflages have been considered ugly and unsightly and have therefore not been used very often. This is rather unfortunate, and to help those who would like to experiment with winter camouflages we include here a reference chart of winter colour schemes that have been seen in historical photographs and other evidence.

Some armoured vehicles used to carry an external box to store spare equipment.

The Chart

This small sample (illustrated overleaf) will help us when we want to make a different model with the security of knowing that all these examples have appeared on actual vehicles.

1. Vertical dull streaks

This effect was produced by the work of the weather on a soluble white base. The original grey paint can be seen and gives the vehicle a dirty white or slightly stained effect.

2. Flaked paint

When a sufficiently thick coat of acrylic paint was applied, it tended to run on large areas.

3. Extreme staining.

The continuous use of a camouflaged vehicle and the passage of time caused almost all of the white paint to disappear while the thick paint in cracks and grooves remained.

4. Speckled.

Anything from a lavatory brush to a handful of fur might have been used in the field to make this nice but very original camouflage. We were able to simulate it with a number 2 or 3 paint brush, painting spots of a regular shape over the whole vehicle.

5. Brush strokes

Finding a broom would be a luxury for a Panzer crew since the vehicle

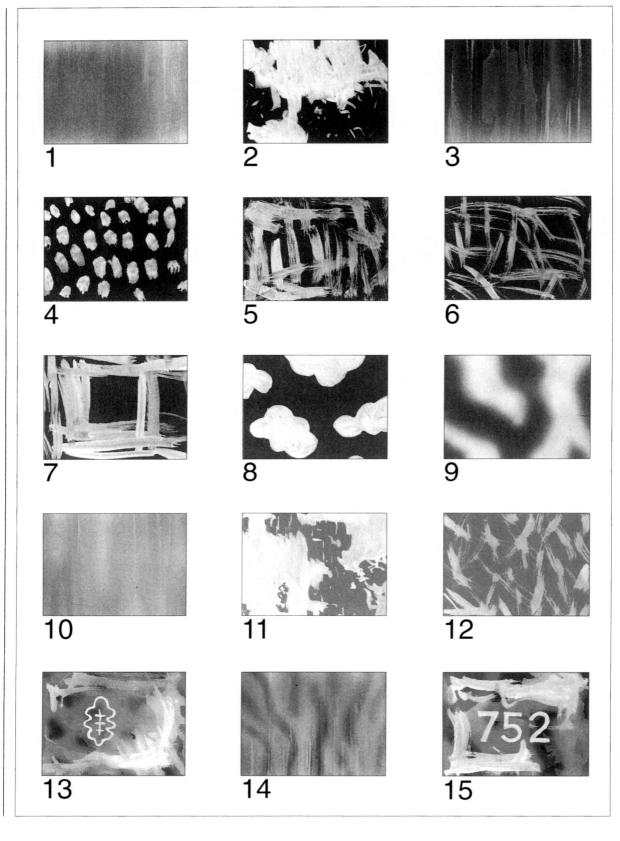

could then be camouflaged rapidly, but it is a nice bit of kit to put on top of the tank! This paint scheme is very rudimentary but was frequently used, particularly on heavy vehicles.

6. Fine detail
In the desert-like steppe conditions the tank crew would use a bunch of reeds or similar plants to make a rudimentary brush.

7. Chequered pattern.
This chequered pattern was used on large vehicles with large numerals painted onto the grey base coat. This ensured that they were clearly visible.

8. Clouds
Some photographs show vehicles with small clouds which were hand-painted onto their entire surface.

9. Bands
Few tanks crews would be able to get their hands on paint spraying equipment but this was without doubt the most efficient means of camouflaging a vehicle.

10 and 11. Wear and tear
Similarly to those vehicles painted in grey, tanks later painted in sand also suffered the consequences of using poor quality paint.

12. Diagonal markings
These were also painted on the sand base coat, using a brush.

13. Irregular markings
By the end of the war camouflage might feature both large and translucent, as well as darker, stained areas.

14. Staining
Heavy rain could dissolve the white paint and leave large areas through which the camouflage could be seen.

15. Re-touching
Thicker paint was used for this.

The Model
It was impossible to show all the various versions in a single model, but we tried to show the most typical ones. For example, we used number 5 for the front section of the driver's armour plating. The rear section of

ABOVE **On some areas, the white paint has practically disappeared and can only be seen in cracks and joints.**

BELOW **The effect of water and dripping mud was reproduced with transparent drawn plastic and silicone.**

ABOVE **The white paint wore away in areas like the track guards and turret roof. These were the place where the crew would step or sit, or rub against while climbing through the hatches.**

RIGHT **Wheels and lower hull sides were often left without white paint since these would in any case be quickly covered in mud.**

the turret corresponds to number 2, with peeling paint. Numbers 1 and 2 have been used for all the horizontal sections. When it comes to painting a different model, simply choose the options which are most appropriate to that particular situation.

Note that real-life vehicles would have been painted almost entirely by hand, and this can be reflected in the model by leaving hairs from the brush on the painted surface, as would occur in real life. Also Humbrol white paint was used so that the drips could be scrubbed onto the surfaces as in real life.

The method of creating white staining can be varied. The front section of the tracks and suspension has a simulated splashed effect.

Treatment of the tank's rear was very important in order to make the camouflage appear credible. The effects of rust, dirt and mud add realism to the model in this area. No special treatment was needed for the white base, but care had to be taken not to darken the camouflage too much.

Mud and Water

This tank is shown having actually crossed a large pool of water produced by a thaw. All the under parts were treated with putty and fine sand and afterwards painted with various Humbrol colours and varnished with satin and gloss varnish to replicate the effect of sticky muddy splashes.

Finally, to reproduce the effect of the water running off the tracks and track guards, transparent drawn plastic covered with clear silicone was used.

The simulated water and mud give the lower parts of the vehicle a semi-glossy finish.

WALKROUND

1 The Germans frequently rebuilt tanks to the latest standard if they were returned to the factory for major repairs. This Ausf. F, preserved at Saumur, is a good example with its late gun mantlet, new sprocket wheels to run on wider tracks, and the added armour on the hull front which was introduced to uparmour the Ausf. H.

4 Early type of idler wheel, designed for the 36cm wide tracks but perfectly able to be used with the 40cm type.

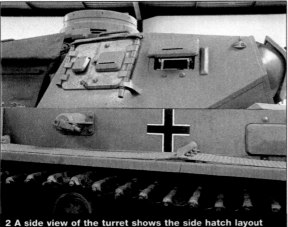

2 A side view of the turret shows the side hatch layout and an open vision port.

5 Rear view of Ausf. F showing early shape of back of the engine deck. Note how a bolted joint runs across it to connect the hull top to its bottom.

3 The second type of sprocket, introduced with new tracks which were 40cm wide. This tank retains its original shock absorbers; the later type had the cylinders at the top and the actuating rod with its cover at the bottom.

6 This is the late type of 40cm track, distinguished by the open loops at the sides of each link.

7 This is the right-hand side's rear return roller. The road wheel tyres show signs of heavy wear.

8 The second type of idler wheel was fitted to PzKpfw IIIs built with the 40cm track as original.

9 Hull-side escape hatch, needed because there was no room for hull-top hatches for the driver and radio operator.

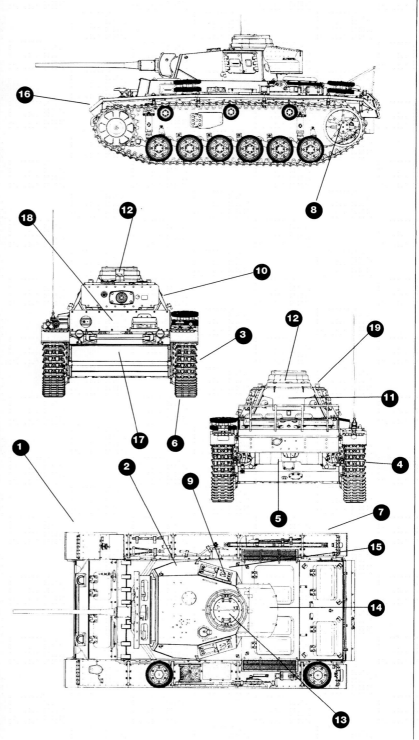

10 The gunner's direct vision port is open here — the gunsight aperture is the small hole beside it. Note also the thickness of the added hull armour and how it stands away from the actual hull front.

13 Commander's cupola showing vision blocks, gunner's seat at the left, front of commander's seat at bottom, and rear of gun recoil guard at top.

11 Flat engine hatches were used up to the Ausf. G. New hatches with raised air vents were introduced for the Ausf. Gs sent to Africa. This tank was also retrofitted with a stowage bin on the turret rear.

14 Ausf. E and F commander's cupola, showing how it was set into a bulge added to the turret rear plate. From late Ausf. Gs onward the turret rear was more vertical and the roof extended back a little, so there was no need for a bulge for the cupola.

12 This improved commander's cupola was introduced with the late Ausf. G.

15 Inside of the turret side hatch; note vision port, a very noticeable feature if you build a model with open hatches.

16 Ausf. N at Aberdeen Proving Ground showing short 7.5cm gun with its different recoil housing. Note how the later type of added hull-front armour was held away from the actual hull by struts at its top.

18 The Ausf N has no added mantlet armour and no cut-out above the driver's visor. Note the stand-off armour fitted to many tanks from Ausf. L onward.

19 Panzer IIIs from Ausf. J onwards used the new hull rear shown here.

17 Aberdeen also has an Ausf. L. This photograph shows the shapes of the late style of added armour for the hull front and gun mantlet.

SCALE DRAWINGS

Ausf. D
Scale 1/48

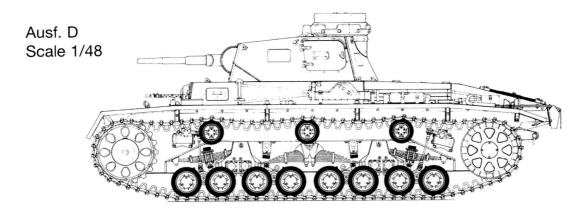

Ausf. F
Scale 1/72

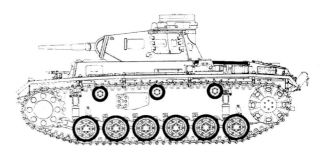

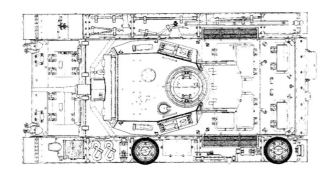

Ausf. G,
four-view
Scale 1/72

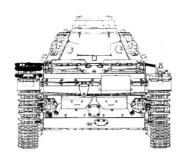

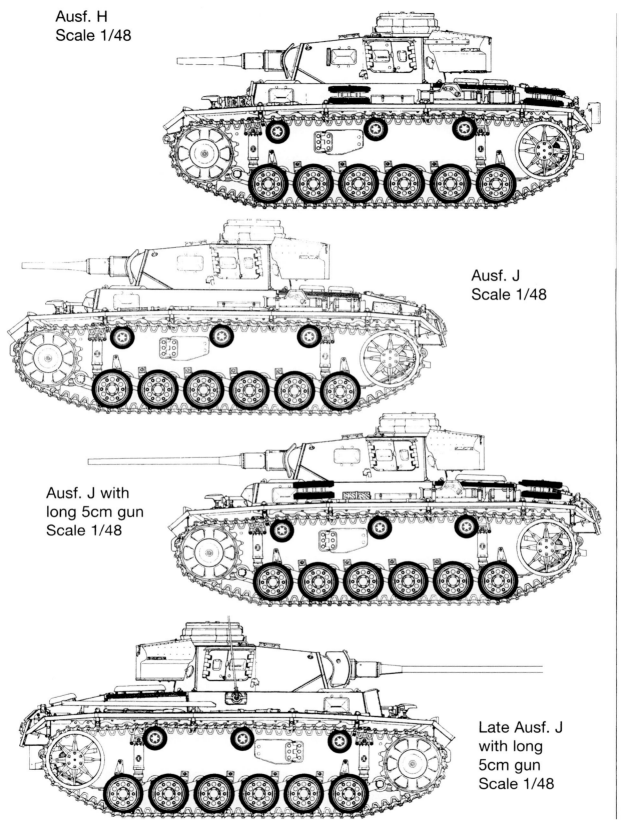

Ausf. H
Scale 1/48

Ausf. J
Scale 1/48

Ausf. J with
long 5cm gun
Scale 1/48

Late Ausf. J
with long
5cm gun
Scale 1/48

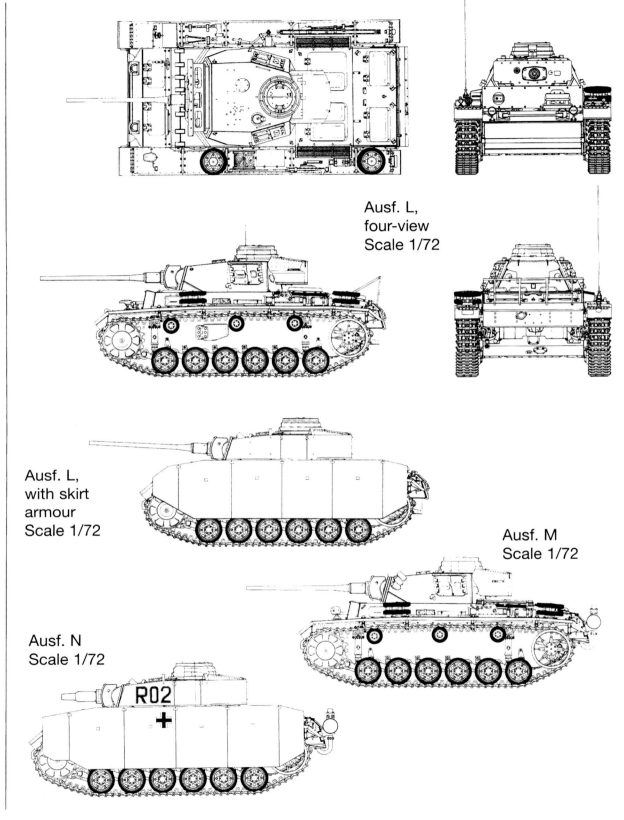

Ausf. L,
four-view
Scale 1/72

Ausf. L,
with skirt
armour
Scale 1/72

Ausf. M
Scale 1/72

Ausf. N
Scale 1/72

CAMOUFLAGE AND MARKINGS

COLOURS AND PATTERNS

The Panzer III served in almost every variation of German camouflage except those only used in the last few months of World War Two, which were applied in the factories after Panzer III production had ceased. The first tanks went into service in plain dark grey, sometimes with earth-brown overstriping. The brown stripes seem to have persisted at least until 1941, though not applied to all tanks. Analysis of photographs shows that the original grey was very dark indeed, but it seems to have become lighter as the war progressed. Photographs exist showing a neat white winter paint scheme applied over the grey as early as 1940/41, but the tanks that served in Russia in the winter of 1941 had a much more patchy appearance. The invasion had been expected to be 'over by Christmas' so no white paint had been provided – also no winter clothing for the troops. The shivering crews camouflaged their Panzers with whatever was to hand, from ordinary whitewash to chalk applied in a variety of ways. Tanks could be seen with a fairly solid whitewash coat on their fronts, the parts expected to be seen by the enemy, with chalk scribbles all round, or even with looted white bedsheets draped over their turrets and hull fronts.

The first *Afrika Korps'* tanks to arrive in North Africa were in their original grey finish, but this was soon covered by sandy dust and very quickly overpainted with whatever sand-tone paints were to hand. Some tanks seem to have been camouflaged with a paste made up from the local earth mixed with water, too. Later tank deliveries, and those of the first ones that survived to be repainted properly, were in a light sand shade and the final deliveries of late 1942 and early 1943 were in a darker sand-brown.

In 1943 the famous three-colour paint scheme was introduced using a basic colour known as *Dunkelgelb*, an ochre tone, with green and red-brown applied over this according to the crew's whim or a unit commander's decision. The extra colours were applied with brushes, spray guns or even with brooms or rags if a quick repaint was needed in the field. The patterns used varied wildly, with no definitive standard

ABOVE **This is an Ausf. J tank adapted to control radio-controlled Borgward chargelayer vehicles. These adapted tanks can easily be distinguished in a side or rear view by the squared-off armoured boxes which held the control radio, replacing the normal stowage box. From the front they can sometimes be picked out by the aerial fitted to the top of the armoured box.**

RIGHT **Panzer III Ausf. G. of 5th Panzer Regiment in 1941. Painted in desert yellow (RAL 8000) over panzer grey (RAL 7027).**

RIGHT **Panzer III Ausf. J of 6th Panzer Regiment, 1st Panzer Division, Russia 1941. Painted in panzer grey (RAL 7027) with irregular blotches in desert brown (RAL 8020).**

FAR RIGHT **Setting the tank in a diorama with not only gives the idea of its size but can also tell a story. Here a PzKpfw III is taking part in the failed German push toward Mortain in 1944. intended to split in half the US offensive along the coast, this vehicle has halted in the ruined town as the attack spluttered to an end.**

being set, but the most common seems to have been a wide overstriping in one or both of the colours although some tanks remained in plain *Dunkelgelb*.

MARKINGS

arkings were of two types: unit symbols applied at front and/or rear and individual tank numbers on the turret sides. Pet names were also sometimes painted on the gun mantlet, the turret side or by a crewman's individual position. The unit symbols came in two types. There were officially laid-down 'code' symbols, mostly composed from horizontal and vertical lines, but some were more complex like the running greyhound of 116th Panzergrenadier Division, and unofficial signs applied to show a unit's pride in itself. Most tanks would show only one of these, but sometimes both the official and unit pride markings appeared together. There is no room here to show them, but some appear in the photographs in this book and many others can be found in the references listed later.

The individual tank numbers were normally carried in threes, the first digit (reading left to right) indicating the company, the second the platoon and the third the individual tank. This system made for quick

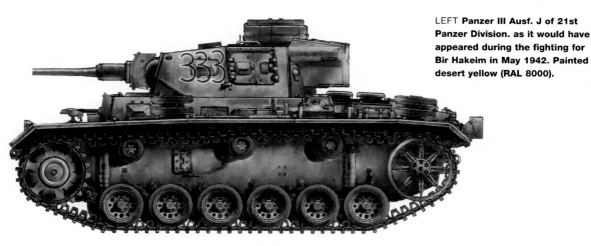

LEFT **Panzer III Ausf. J of 21st Panzer Division. as it would have appeared during the fighting for Bir Hakeim in May 1942. Painted desert yellow (RAL 8000).**

LEFT **Panzer III Ausf. H of 3rd Panzer Division in 1941. This example shows the markings for 1st Company, 2nd Platoon, 2nd Tank. Painted in panzer grey (RAL 7027).**

identification when a commander wanted to issue orders – for instance '123 go left, 125 go right, 122 straight ahead', or 'tank 323, enemy tank in ambush to your left, proceed slowly and keep his attention while I work round him'. The numbers were usually quite large, and could be painted in white, yellow, red, blue, or black. Contrasting outlines were often applied, and the numbers were also seen in outline form. Some units used different colours to identify their companies, while others used a single colour for all their tanks.

RIGHT **Again, a diorama tells a story. Here we see some very cold soldiers restocking with ammunition while snow lies on the ground. The impression is increased by the way the commander has to huddle down into his cupola, out of the wind as far as he can get while still keeping watch.**

BELOW **Panzer III Ausf. L. of 5th SS Panzer Division (*Wiking*) in 1942. Painted in desert yellow (RAL 8000) with blotches of desert brown (RAL 8020).**

BELOW **Panzer III Ausf. M of Panzer Regiment 11, 6th Panzer Division, in 1943. This example is painted in desert yellow (RAL 8000) with blotches of desert brown (RAL 8020) and grey green (RAL 7008).**

MODEL ROUND-UP

As mentioned in the Introduction, there are quite a few Panzer III kits available in various scales, and manufacturers have produced a variety of accessories, upgrades and conversions to go with them. Although space doesn't allow an exhaustive list, those described in the table overleaf are the most easily available.

Accessories, Upgrades and Conversions

Unlike the kits, accessory and upgrade sets can be hard to find. UK stockists are given below. Readers from other countries should study the the model magazines of their home country for stockists outside the UK.

Aber makes a range of etched metal accessories including sets for kits of the Panzer III Ausf. J, L, M/N and the Beobachtungswagen H. They make separate accessory sets giving the hull and turret skirt armour, and also a simple set with just the engine air intake grilles, which is very useful if you only want to replace the plastic grilles that come in some kits without adding any extra detail. The UK agent is Historex Agents, telephone: 01304 206720, email: Sales@historex-agents.demon.co.uk.

Cromwell Models has an excellent resin conversion set to build the Befehlspanzer III Ausf. D1 with its very different suspension. They can be reached at telephone: 0141 402 4016, email: cromwell@xs4all.nl.

Eduard is another etched metal set maker with products for the Panzer III, specifically Revell's Ausf. J, Tamiya's new Ausf. L and even a set to improve Tamiya's old Ausf. M/N kit. If you can't find them locally, the UK agent is LSA Models, telephone: 01273 705420, email: lsamodels@mc.mail.com.

Dragon has produced its own track sets for those wishing to change those in their own or other kits. These are available for both the early 36cm-wide and the more common 40cm-wide tracks. A set of *Ostketten* winter tracks with extended connectors is out of production at the moment but can still be found by searching around.

Friulmodel offers white metal link-to-link tracks for both the early 36cm and the more common 40cm Panzer III tracks, as well as sprockets for the early and late track types. All are white metal castings. The tracks were originally produced with jaws to be pressed closed over pins

BELOW **Dragon's kit of the Ausf. G includes the extra water cans carried by many** *Afrika Korps* **tanks, together with markings for a tank of the 5th Light Division. A set of decals for a Panzer III G of 2nd Panzer Division in Russia is also included.**

Dragon's Panzer III Ausf. E comes with markings for the Fall of France era, or the campaigns in the Balkans and Greece in 1941. It also includes an etched metal fret for the engine air intake grilles.

KITS

Maker	Variant	Rating	
1/76 & 1/72 scale			
Matchbox	Ausf. L, now apparently released by Revell	**	A
Esci	Ausf. M	**	A
1/48 scale			
Bandai	Ausf. M, some internal details	**	A
1/35 scale			
Dragon	Ausf. E	***	A
	Ausf. G *Afrika Korps*	***	A
	Ausf. H	***	A
	Ausf. H Tauchpanzer with diving tank parts	***	A
	Ausf. H Beobachtungswagen artillery observation tank	***	A
	Ausf. J	***	A
	Ausf. K Panzerbefehlswagen command tank	***	A
	Ausf. M and N in one kit	***	A
	Flammpanzer flamethrower tank	***	A
	Panzer III command tank and Borgward chargelayer	***	A
Gunze Sangyo	Ausf. J and L in one kit	**	B
	Ausf. N	***	B
Revell	Ausf. J	***	A
Tamiya	Ausf. L	***	A
	Ausf. M and N in one kit, with poor figures	**	A

KEY

Symbol	Meaning
***	a top quality kit
**	medium quality
*	less detailed
A	simple enough for a beginner to build successfully
B	suitable for moderately experienced modellers
C	for experts only

Note: *The marking of kits and accessories as simple enough for a beginner is not intended to devalue them in expert eyes, just to show which ones inexperienced modellers can tackle and produce good results from.*

cast into the next link, but are now a new style which uses pins cut from supplied wire to join the link. Both types are easy to use, but note that the early type can stretch or come undone under their own weight. Available from Historex Agents in the UK.

Jordi Rubio is an established maker of turned aluminium gun barrels, which simply replace the plastic parts, and produces some for the Panzer III. They are available from LSA Models in the UK and from armour-model shops in the US and other countries.

Model Kasten of Japan also has link-to-link track sets for the Panzer III. These are in plastic and are easy to assemble. Accurate Armour is the UK agent for Model Kasten, telephone: 01475 743955, email: enquiries@accurate-armour.com.

New **Connections** of Germany has turned aluminium gun barrels for both the short and long 5cm guns. Historex Agents is a stockist for these in the UK.

On The Mark Models is another maker of etched metal sets and has set TMP-3509 for the Panzer III. The company can be contacted at PO Box 663, Louisville, KY 80027, USA.

There are three resin interior sets for the Panzer III from **Verlinden Productions**. A simple engine and transmission set is available for modellers who want to show these items out of a tank in a workshop scene. For use inside a model they have a complete engine compartment for any Panzer III and a fighting compartment interior specifically for Tamiya's Ausf. L. For the outside of a model they offer a set of jerrycans and stowage racks giving several of the patterns of rack commonly carried by the Panzer III. Larger model shops often stock the Verlinden range, but you can also mail-order from Historex Agents in the UK and from many stockists in other countries.

LEFT **The Tauchpanzer III was a modified version of the Panzer III Ausf. H, and Dragon produced a second Ausf. H kit with the necessary modifications and extra parts. Although the 'diving tank' was intended for the invasion of Britain its actual use was in the invasion of Russia, and the kit comes with markings for a tank used in the crossing of the River Bug in 1941.**

LEFT **This is the 1988 Gunze Sangyo kit of the Panzer III Ausf. N with its short 7.5cm gun. Nowadays it is regarded as a collector's item, but if you find one at a reasonable price it is still worth building — though some of the white metal parts will be better replaced by their plastic equivalents from Dragon or Tamiya.**

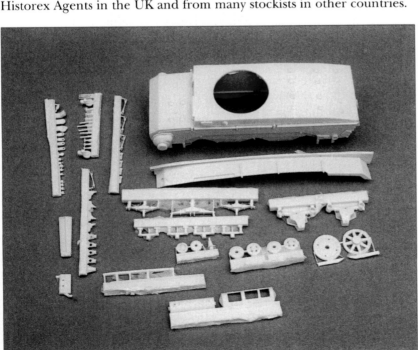

LEFT **Cromwell Models makes a very nice conversion to turn Dragon's Panzer III Ausf. E into the Befehlspanzer III Ausf. D1, a command tank built on the early Ausf. D chassis with a quite different appearance. Here is the replacement hull with a few of the other parts.**

REFERENCES

BIBLIOGRAPHY

There are fewer books about the Panzer III than you might expect, given its service all through World War Two and the number built. The best single reference for English-speakers is Osprey's New Vanguard 27, *Panzerkampfwagen III Medium Tank 1936–1944*, by Bryan Perrett and Mike Badrocke, ISBN 1-85532-453. This gives a technical history of all the variants, notes on wartime service, a selection of good photographs and colour plates with notes on camouflage and markings. However, coverage of the Flammpanzer III is limited and for more information on this version you need New Vanguard 15, *Flammpanzer, German Flamethrowers 1941–45* by Tom Jentz and Hilary Doyle, ISBN 1-85532-547-0. This has quite a lot about the Flammpanzer III and its combat use, including good photographs and colour plates.

Another book in English is *PzKpfw III In Action* by Bruce Culver, published by Squadron/Signal Publications Inc, ISBN 0-89747-199-7. This is less of a text reference and more of a photobook, with many photographs showing Panzer III variants, a centre spread of colour plates, and several scale plans and detail sketches. It makes a good supplement to the New Vanguard books for those wanting more ideas for colours and markings for their models.

The 'bible' for the Panzer III is *Der Panzerkampfwagen III Und Seine Abarten* by Walter J. Speilberger, published by Motorbuch Verlag, ISBN 3-87943-336-4. As you might guess from the title, it is in German but not too hard for non-German readers to puzzle out with the help of a good German/English dictionary. It includes descriptions of all the Ausführungen with the best available photographs of the early versions with their running gear so different to the main production types. Several experiments on the Panzer III chassis are also covered, together with information about the self-propelled guns derived from the Panzer III.

The final suggestion for Panzer III modellers is *Achtung Panzer, No. 2, Panzerkampfwagen III*, published by Dai Nippon Kaiga, ISBN 4-499-20578-6. Although its text is principally in Japanese all the captions for the many photographs, detail sketches and plans are also translated into English and it covers all the gun tanks, command and observation versions of the Panzer III in detail. The photographs include in-service shots from German archives, detailed close-ups showing features of surviving tanks, and even interior photographs of Panzer IIIs in museums. This book will need to be sought in specialist military bookshops, but Accurate Armour (contact details in Model Round-Up Chapter) also stocks the *Achtung Panzer* series in the UK.

THE PANZER III IN MUSEUMS

Considering the numbers of all the various versions which were built, few Panzer IIIs have survived to be seen in museums, though some also remain in private collections.

The **Tank Museum** at Bovington has an Ausf. J in running order, which makes an impressive sight when it appears in the arena at special display days. The Museum also has an Ausf. N which has been cut open so that you can look into it. Although some parts are missing, the major items can still all be seen. The contact address is The Tank Museum, Bovington, Dorset, BH20 6JG, telephone: 01929 405096 and email: admin@tankmuseum.co.uk.

Panzer III Ausf. F in the Saumur Musée des Blindes.

The **Musée des Blindes** at Saumur in France also has a Panzer III, this one an Ausf. F which was uparmoured by the Germans. The museum can be contacted at Musée des Blindes, 1043 route de Fontrevaud, 49000-Saumur, France, telephone: 021 41 53 0699, email: museedesblindes @symphonie-fai.fr.

Several Panzer IIIs can be seen in Germany. The **Motor Technik Museum** at Bad Oeynhausen has an Ausf. E and the **Panzermuseum** at Munster has an Ausf. L restored to full running order. The **Auto und Technik Museum** at Sinsheim has an Ausf. N and the only remaining Flammpanzer III can be found at the **Wehrtechnische Studiensammlung** in Koblenz.

The **Aberdeen Proving Ground Museum** in Maryland, USA, has a late Ausf. J and the **Patton Museum of Cavalry and Armou**r at Fort Knox, Kentucky, has a rebuilt Ausf. F which has been restored to running order, an Ausf. L and an Ausf. N. The Patton Museum can be contacted at PO Box 208, Fort Knox, KY 04121-0208, USA, telephone: (502) 624-3812, email: MUSEUM@ftknox-emh.army.mil.

PANZER III ON THE WEB

There are no websites dedicated to the Panzer III, though several sites have extensive information about the tank. Achtung Panzer, for example, is about German tanks in general and has a page for the Panzer III at www.achtungpanzer.com/pz8.htm. Similar sites can be found through Tony Matteliano's Scale Modelling Index, www.buffnet.net/~tonym/models.htm, a highly recommended resource for finding reference sites and other information for all kinds of modelling. Modellers wishing to make a destroyed Panzer III as shown on pages 30–39 will find excellent reference photographs in the archive section of Mike Kendall's AFV Interiors website at www.kithobbyist.com/AFVInteriors.

Several tank discussion groups on the web are worth a visit, too, where you are welcome to pose questions and get answers. These groups include many well-known modellers and tank experts. Missing Links is at www.missing-lynx.com, Track-Link at www.track-link.net, AFV News at www.mo-money.com/AFV-news, and Hyperscale at www.hyperscale.com. Genuine enquiries are welcome at all of these.

The Achtung Panzer website features a Panzer III on its front page.